I0467770

John's Canvas Prints – Sample Floral Collection

Photography

John A. Messmer, Jr.

www.createspace.com
Scott's Valley, CA 95066
USA

Visit http://www.johnscanvassprints.imagekind.com to order canvas prints of these beautiful photographs and others for your home or office. Many choices and payment options are available. Inform your friends on social media.

John's Canvas Prints – Sample Floral Collection
All Rights Reserved
Photos Copyright © 2014 by John A. Messmer, Jr.

No part of this book may be reproduced or transmitted in any form or by any means, electronic or mechanical, including photocopying, recording, or by an information storage and retrieval system without permission in writing from the author.

Printed in the United States of America

First Printing

For more information or to order additional books, please contact:

www.createspace.com
100 Enterprise Way
Suite A200
Scotts Valley, CA 95066
USA

Dedicated to flower lovers.

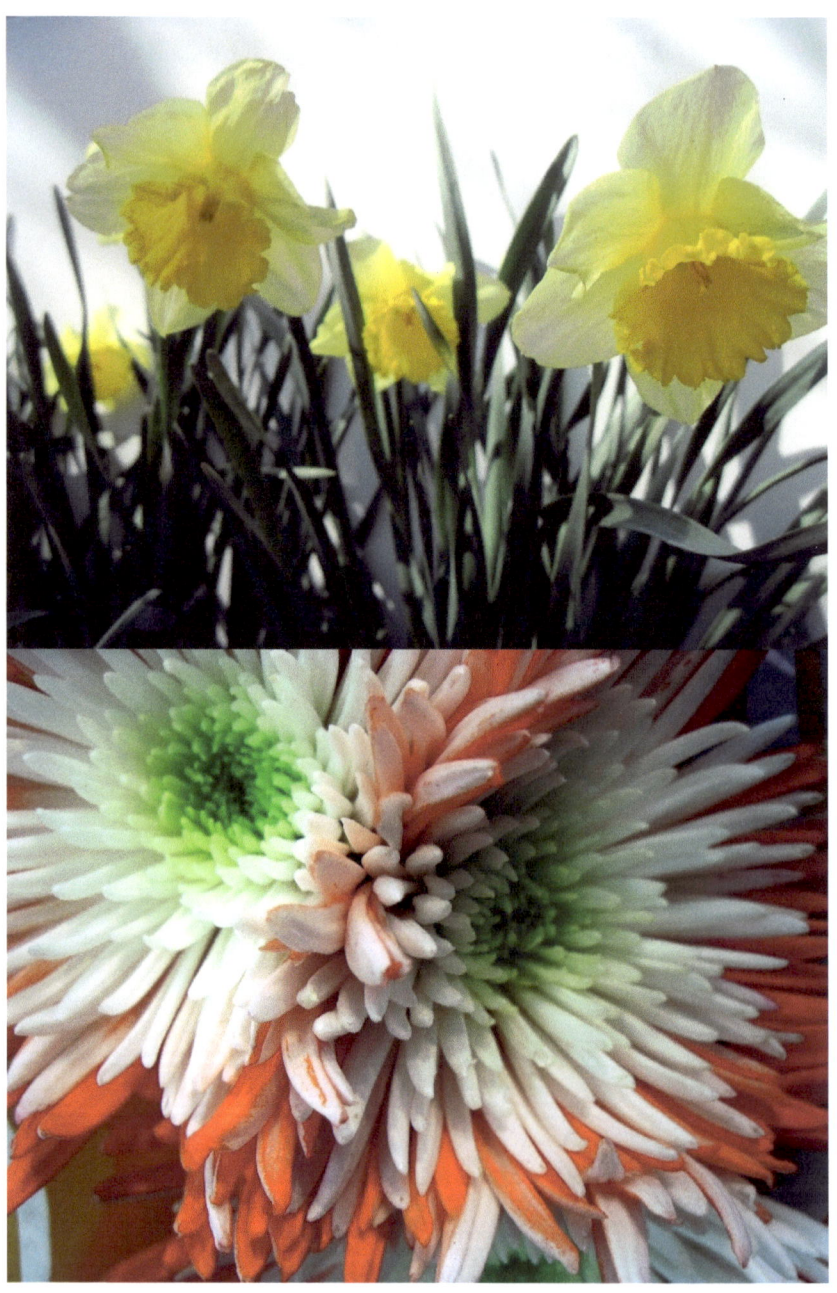

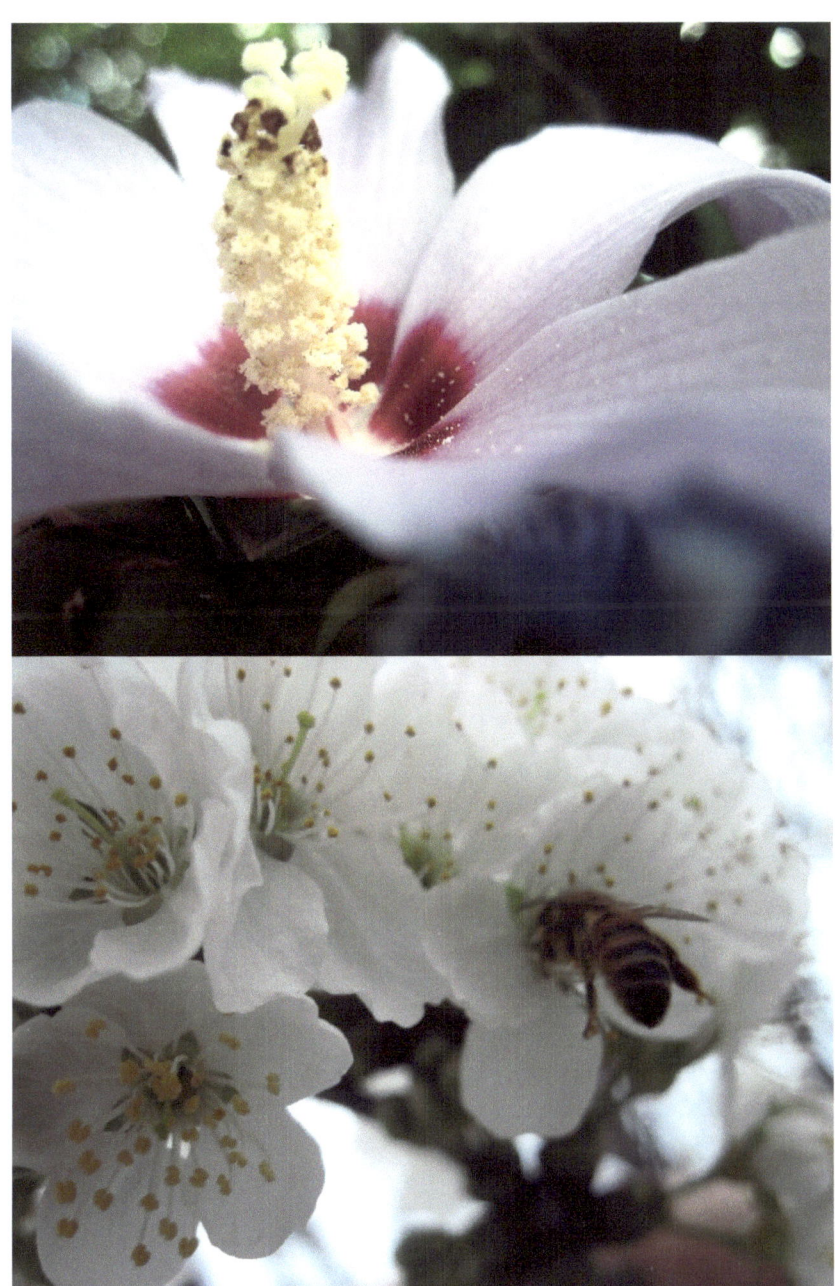

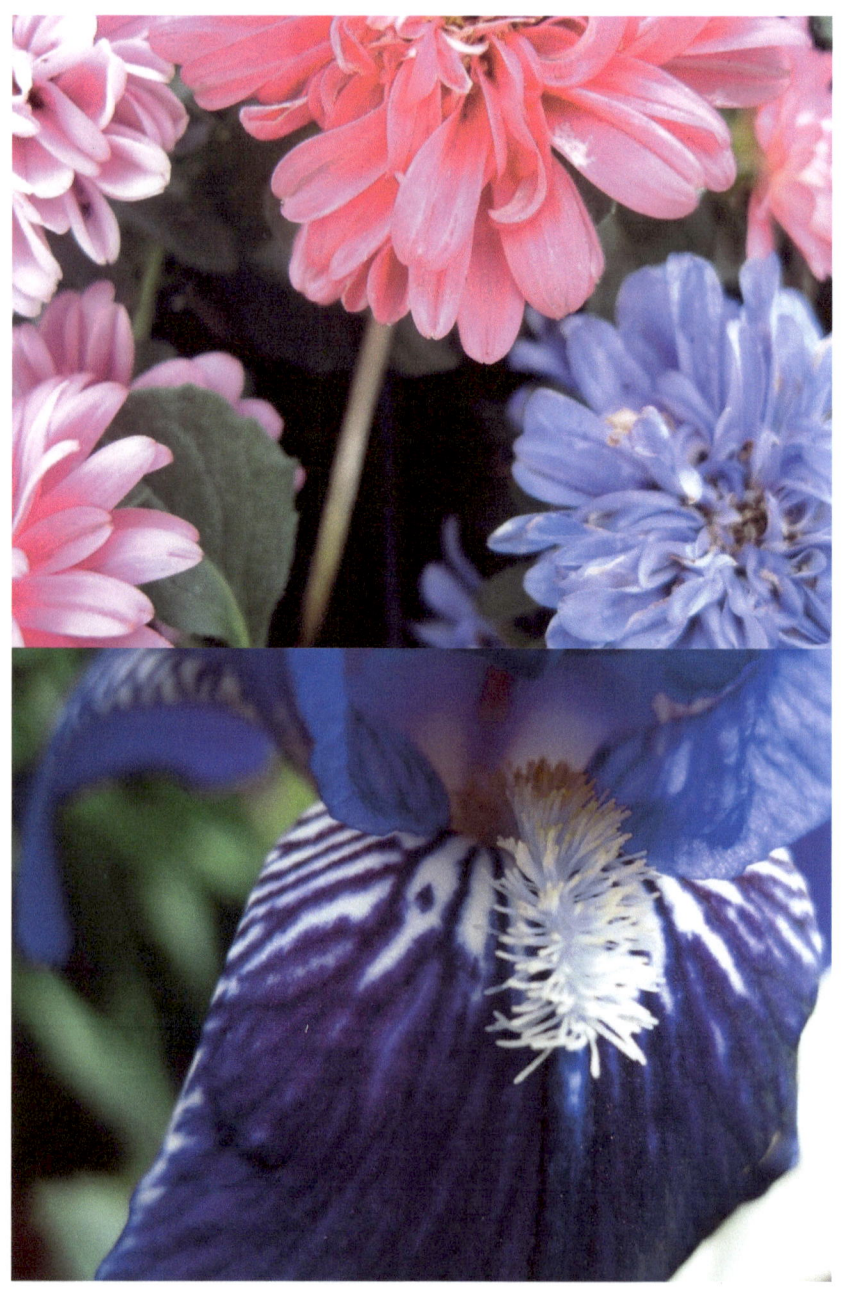

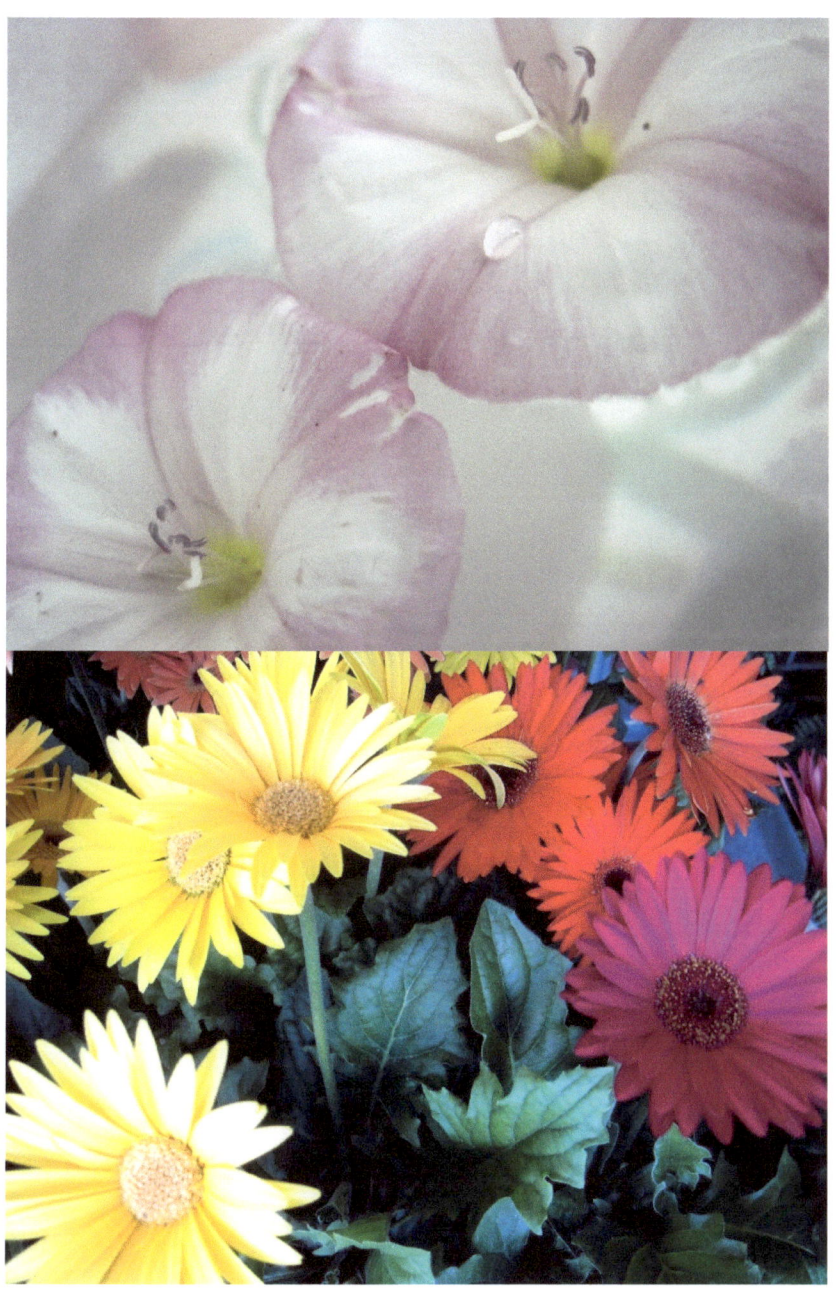

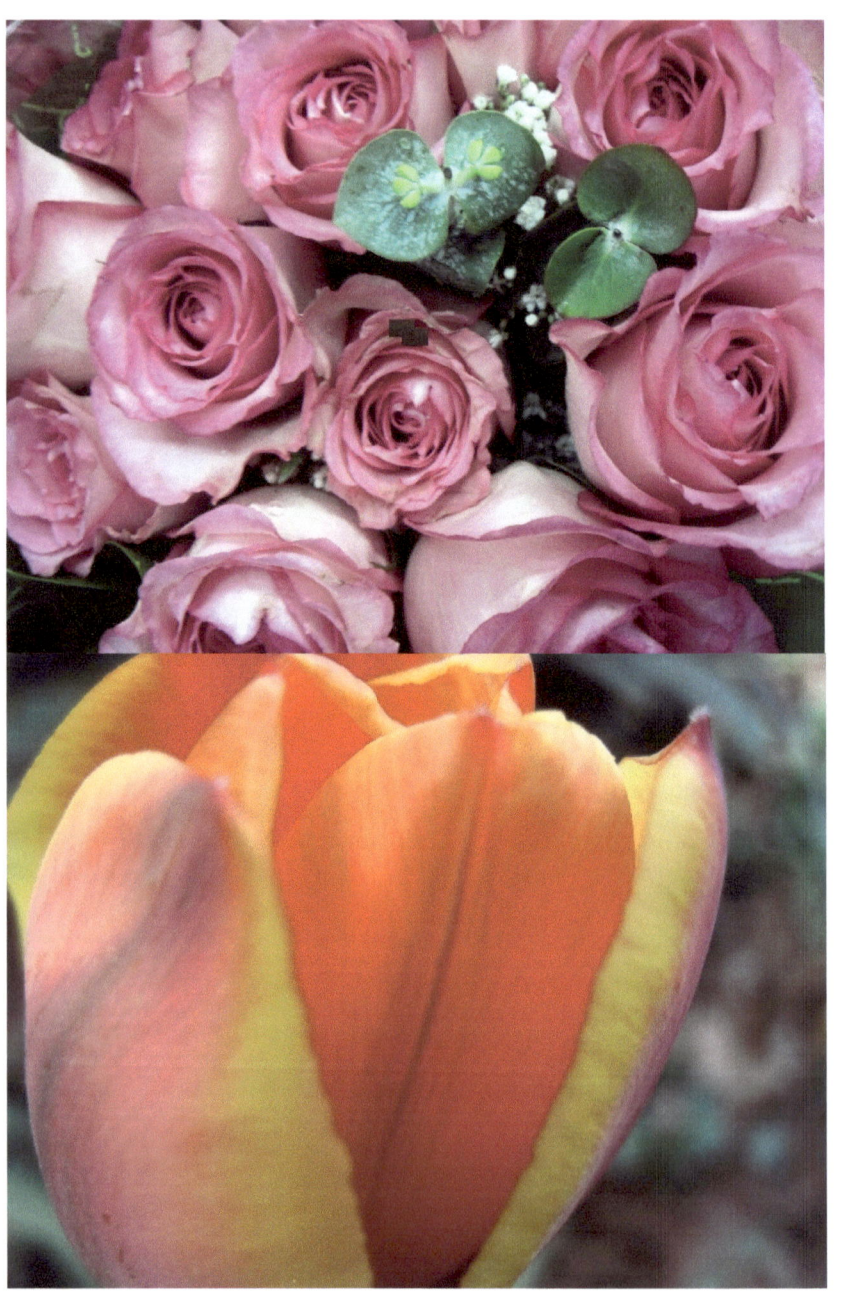

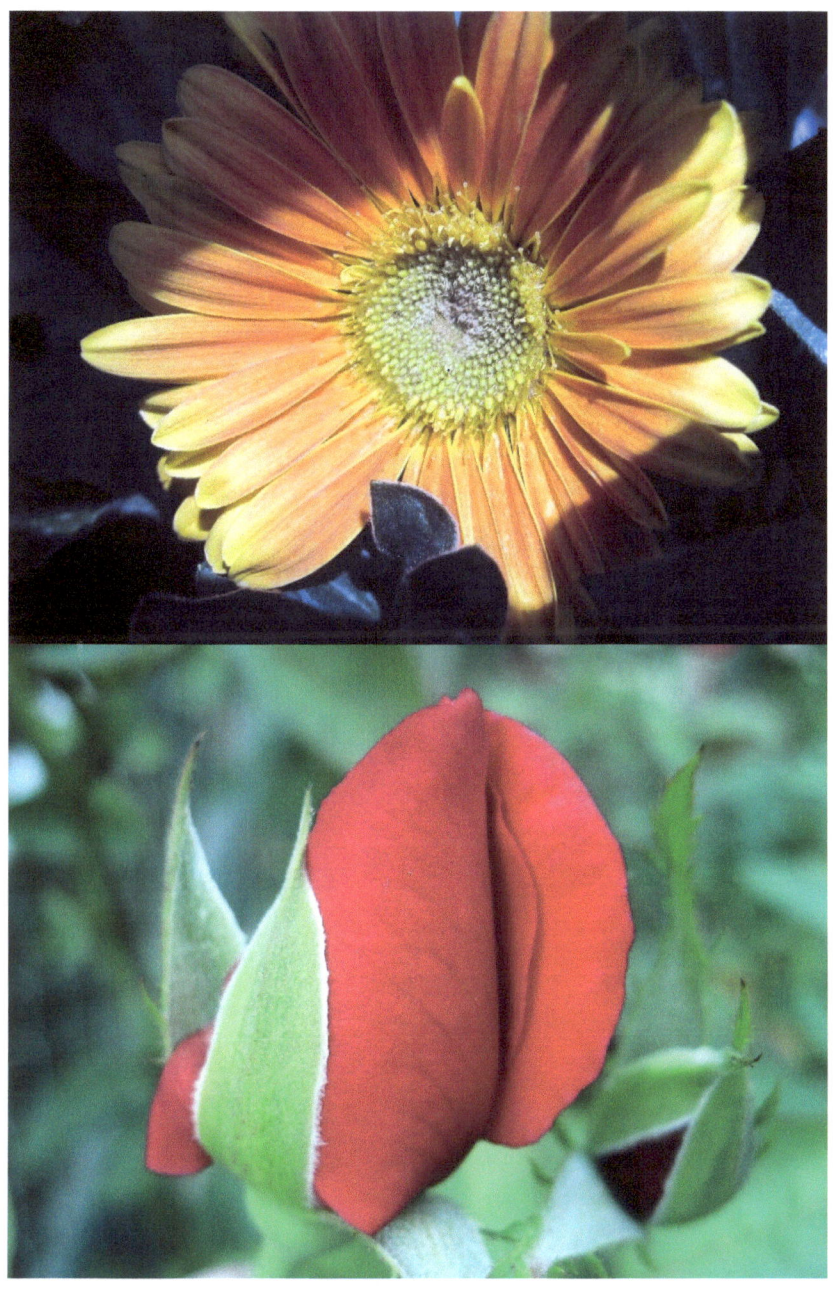

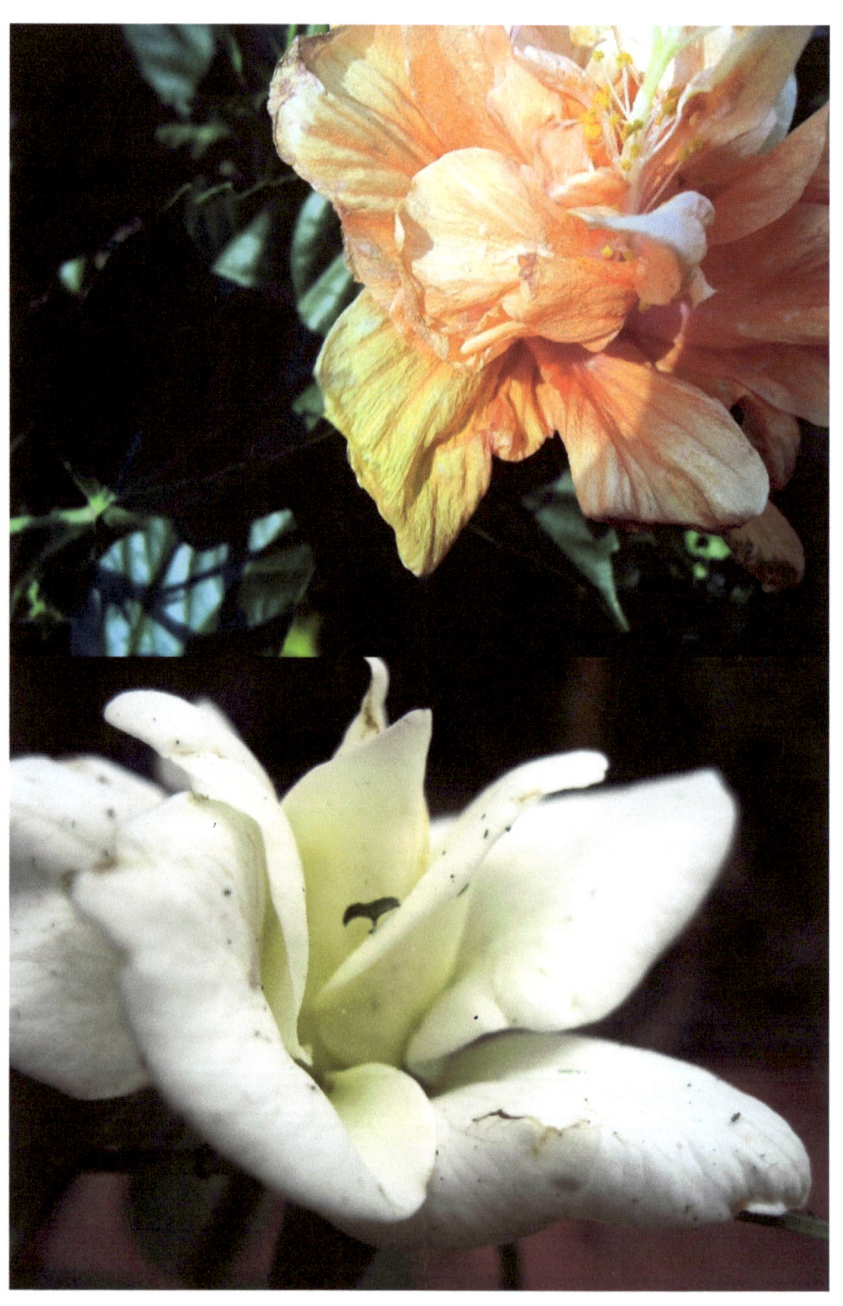

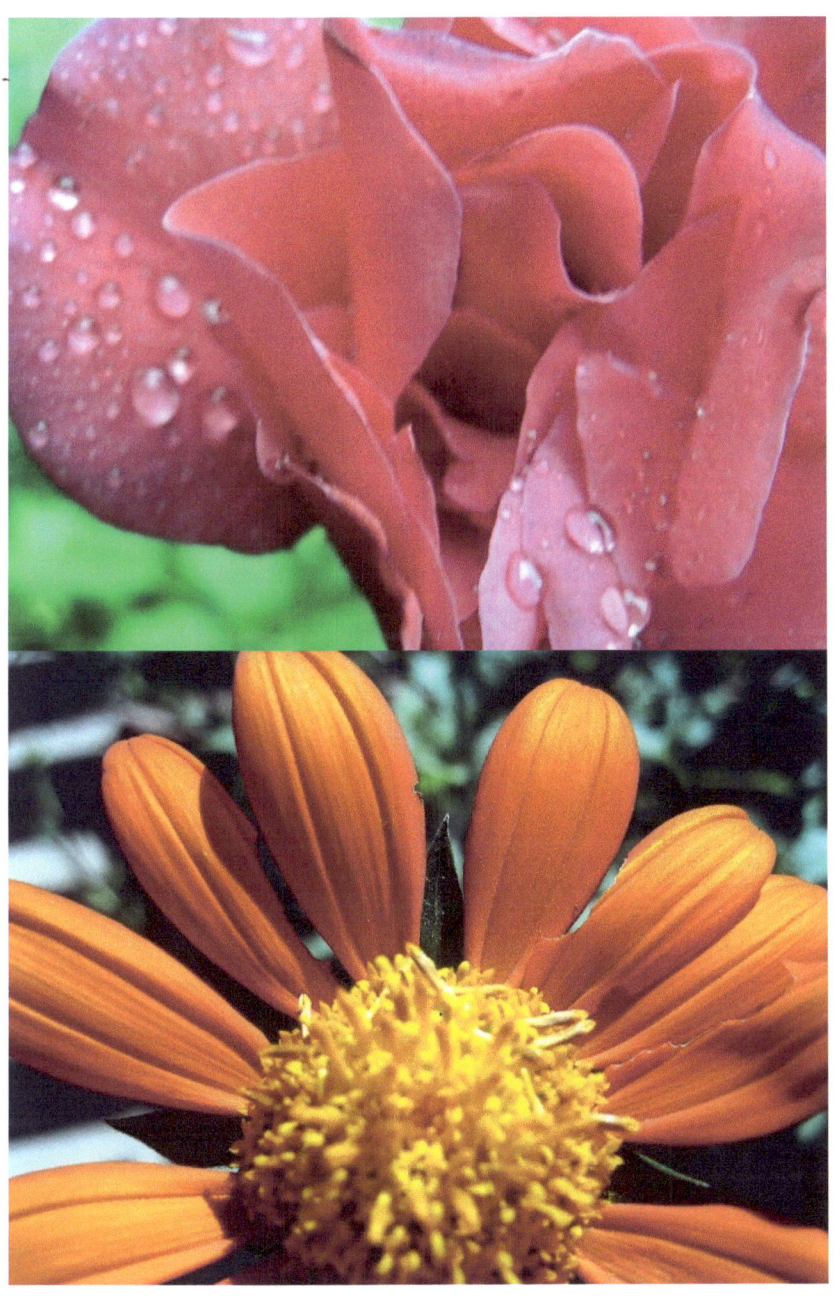

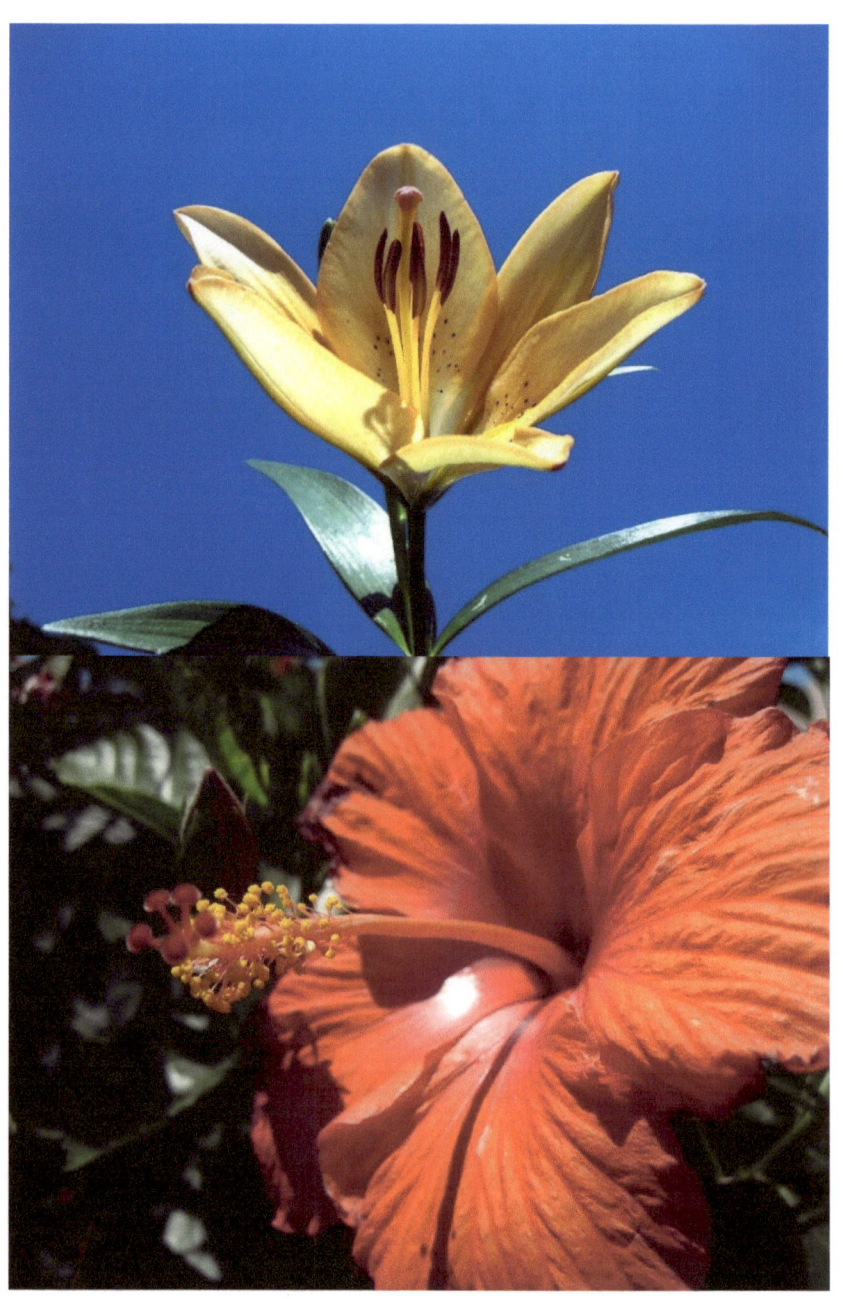

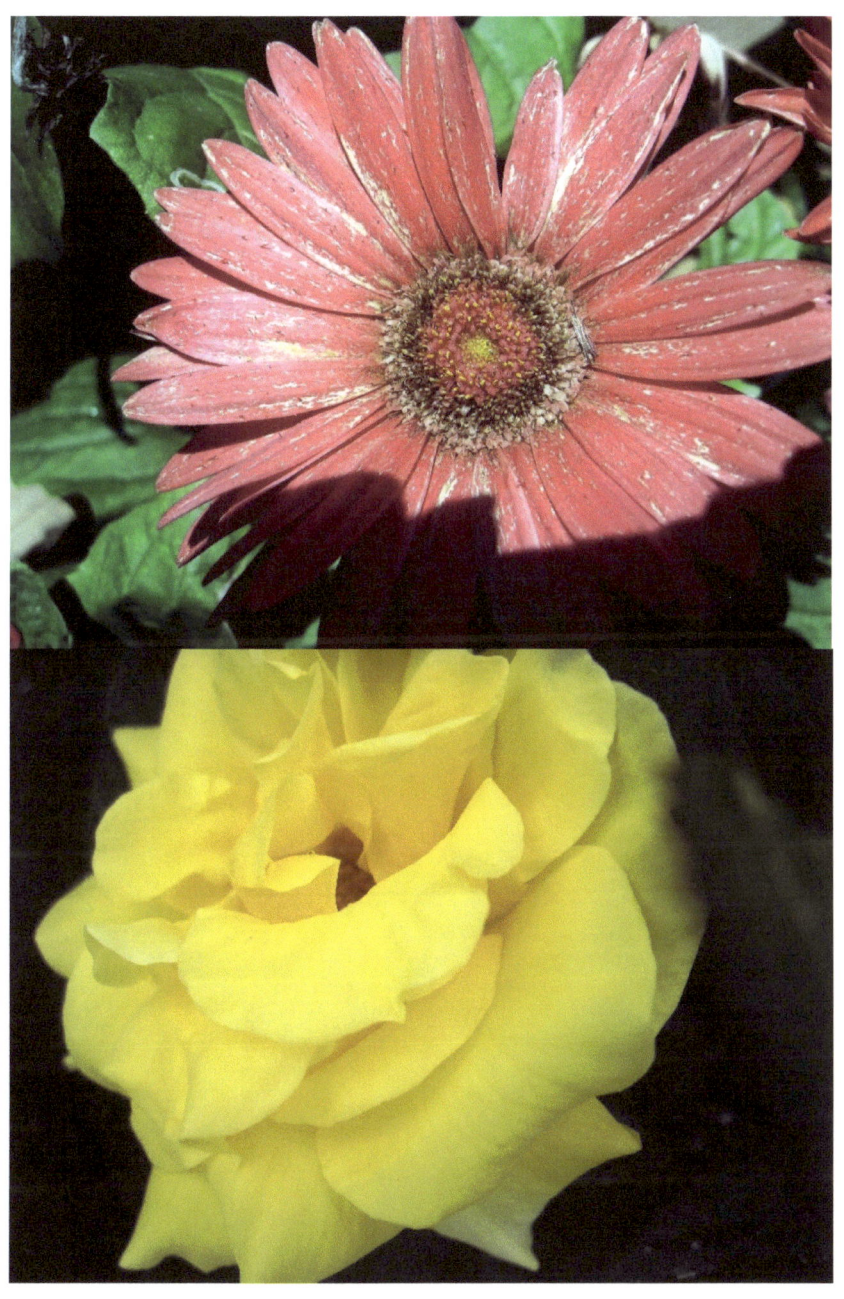

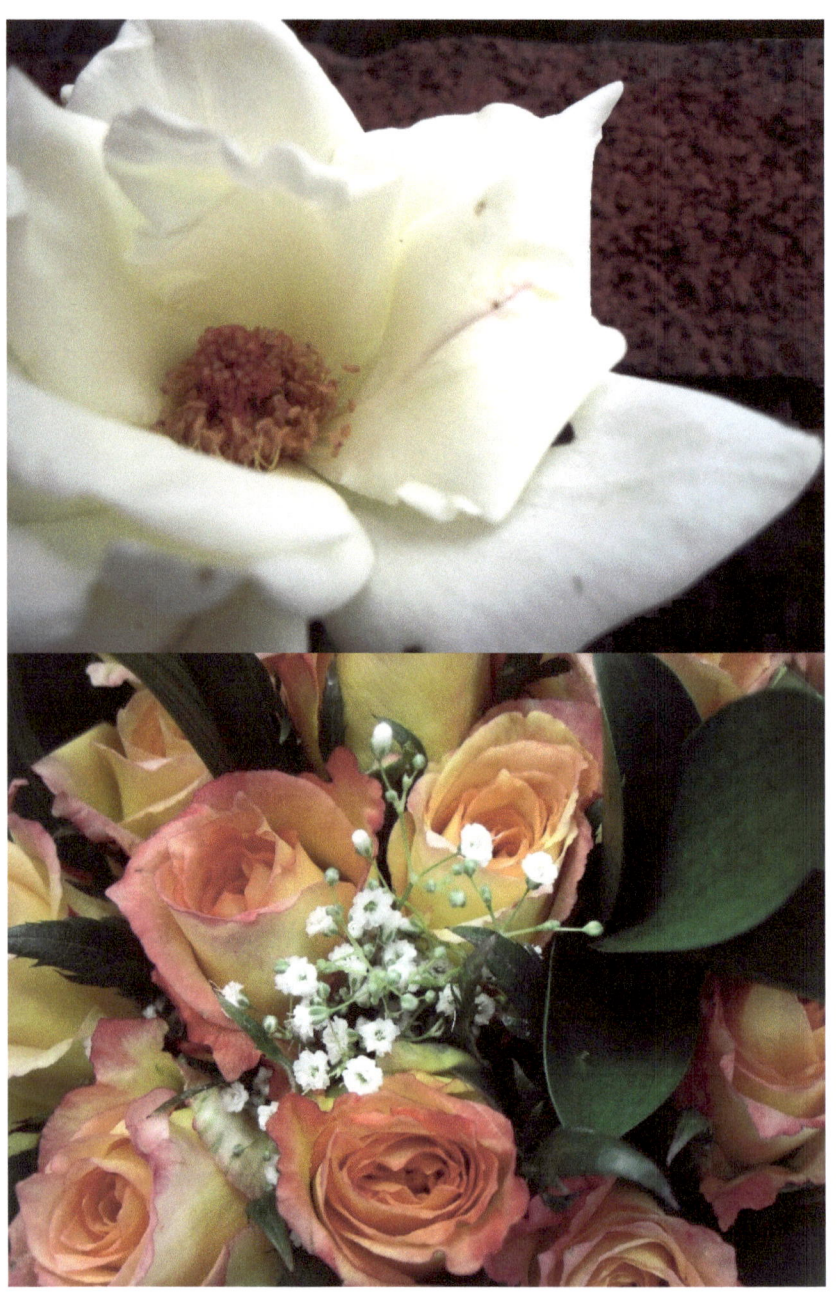

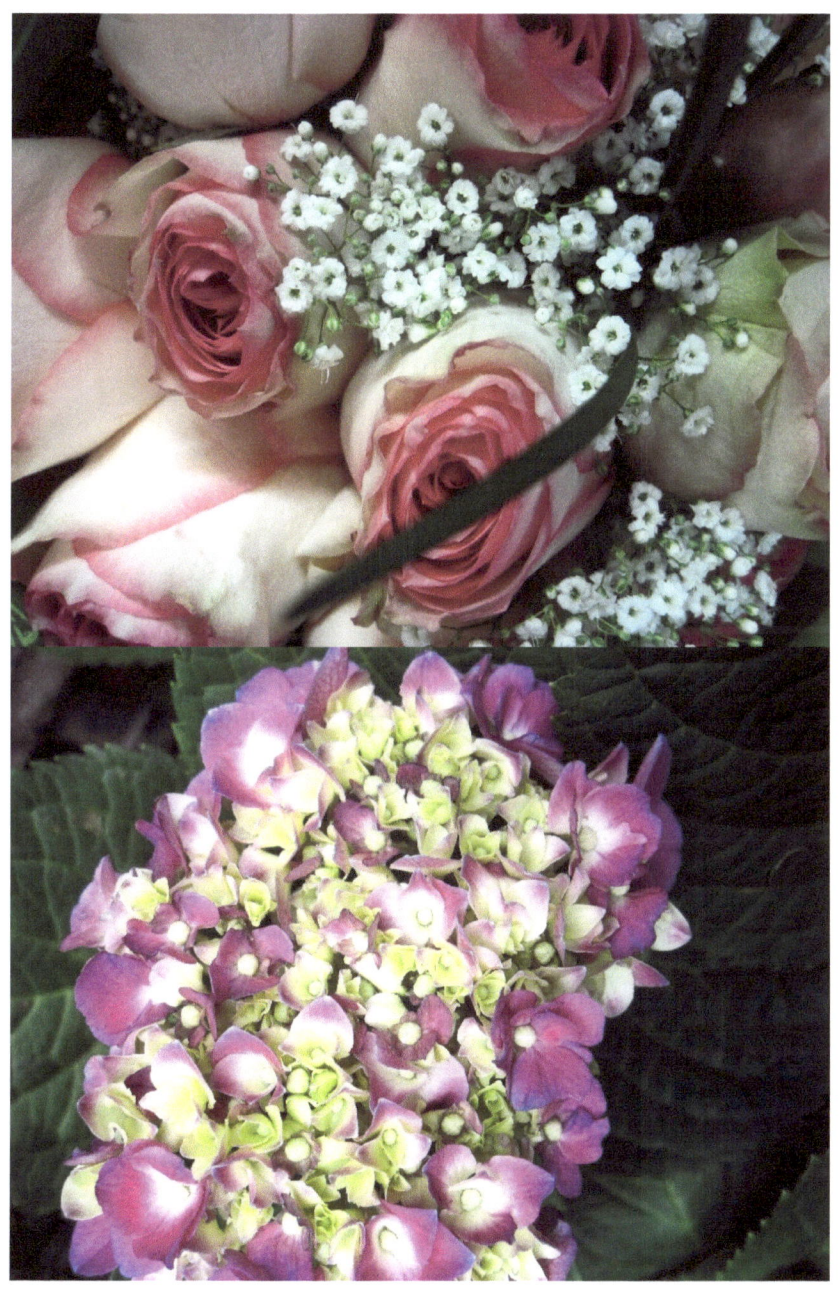

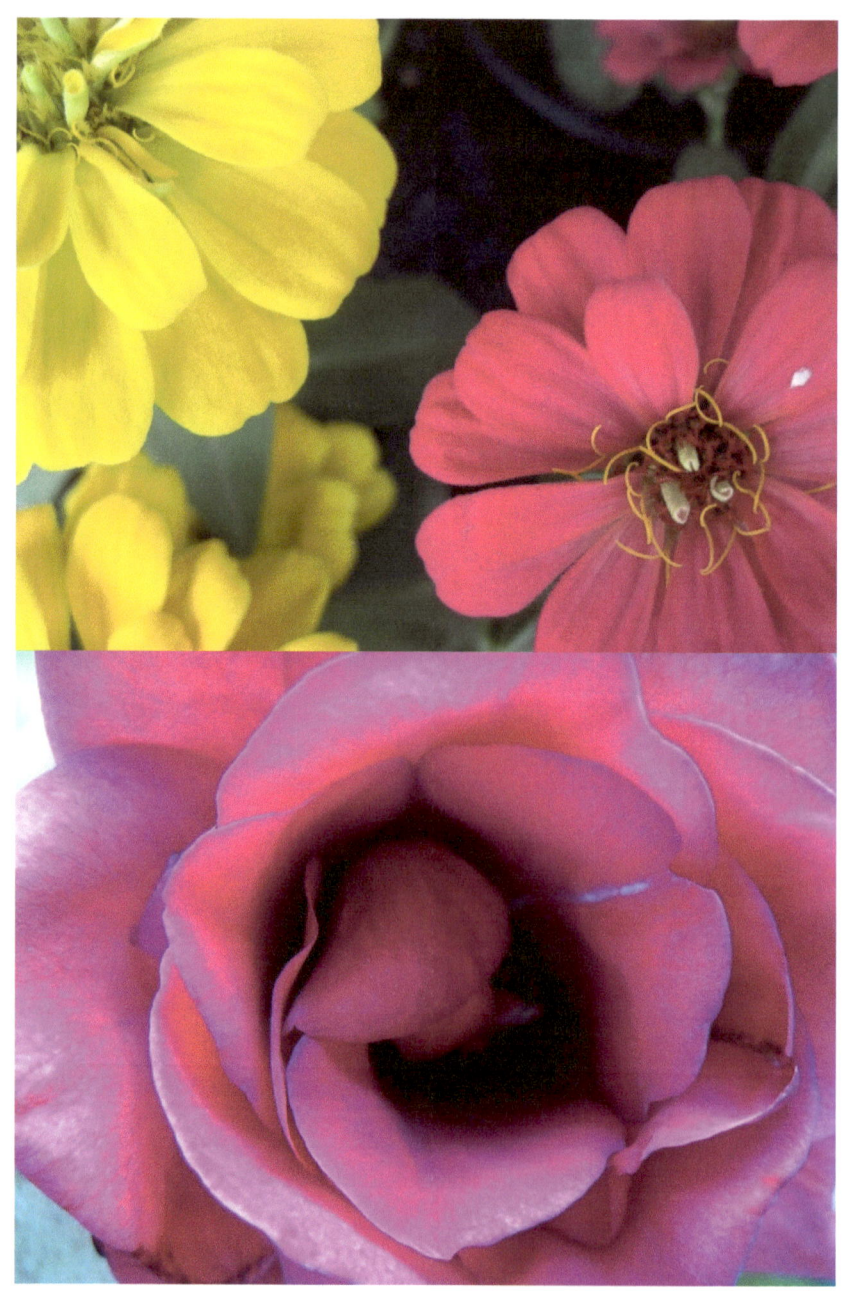

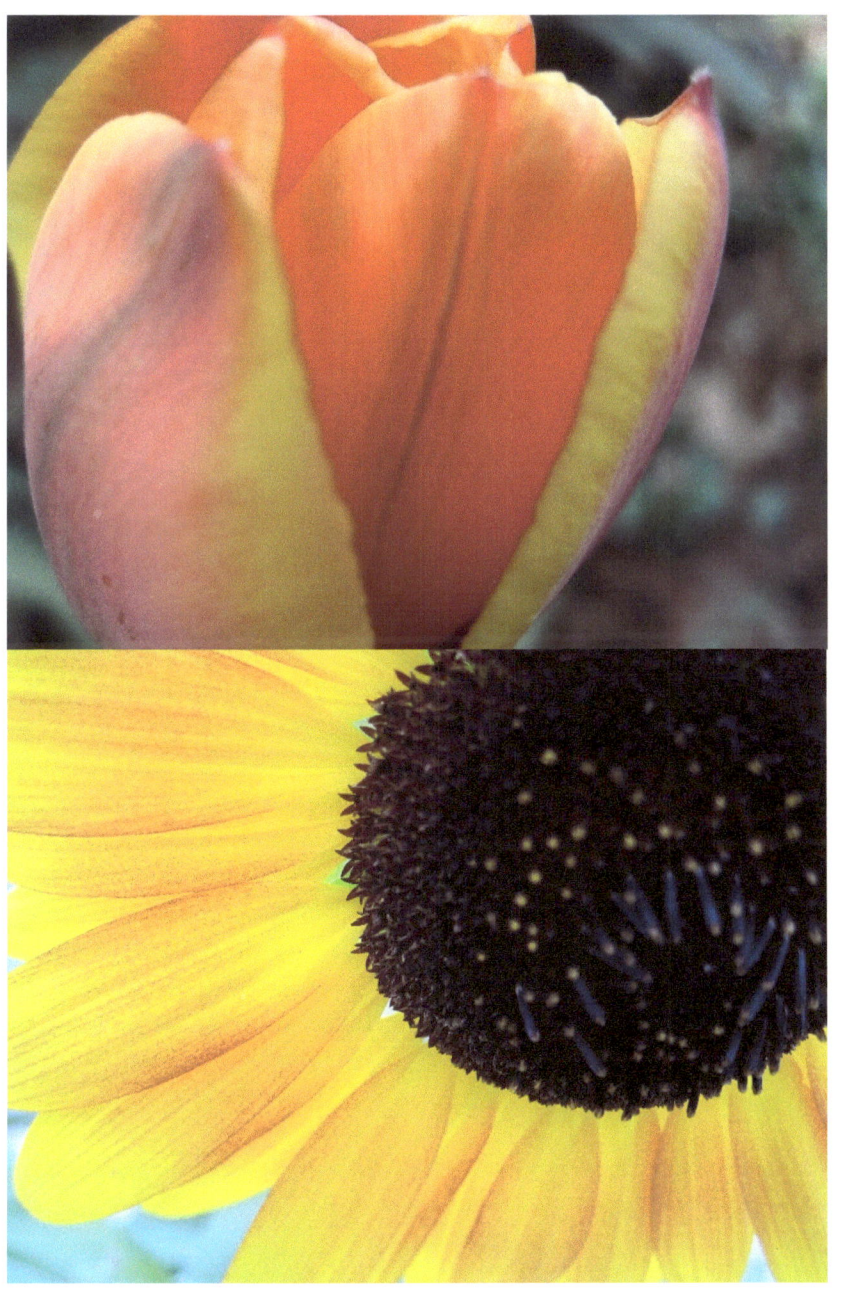

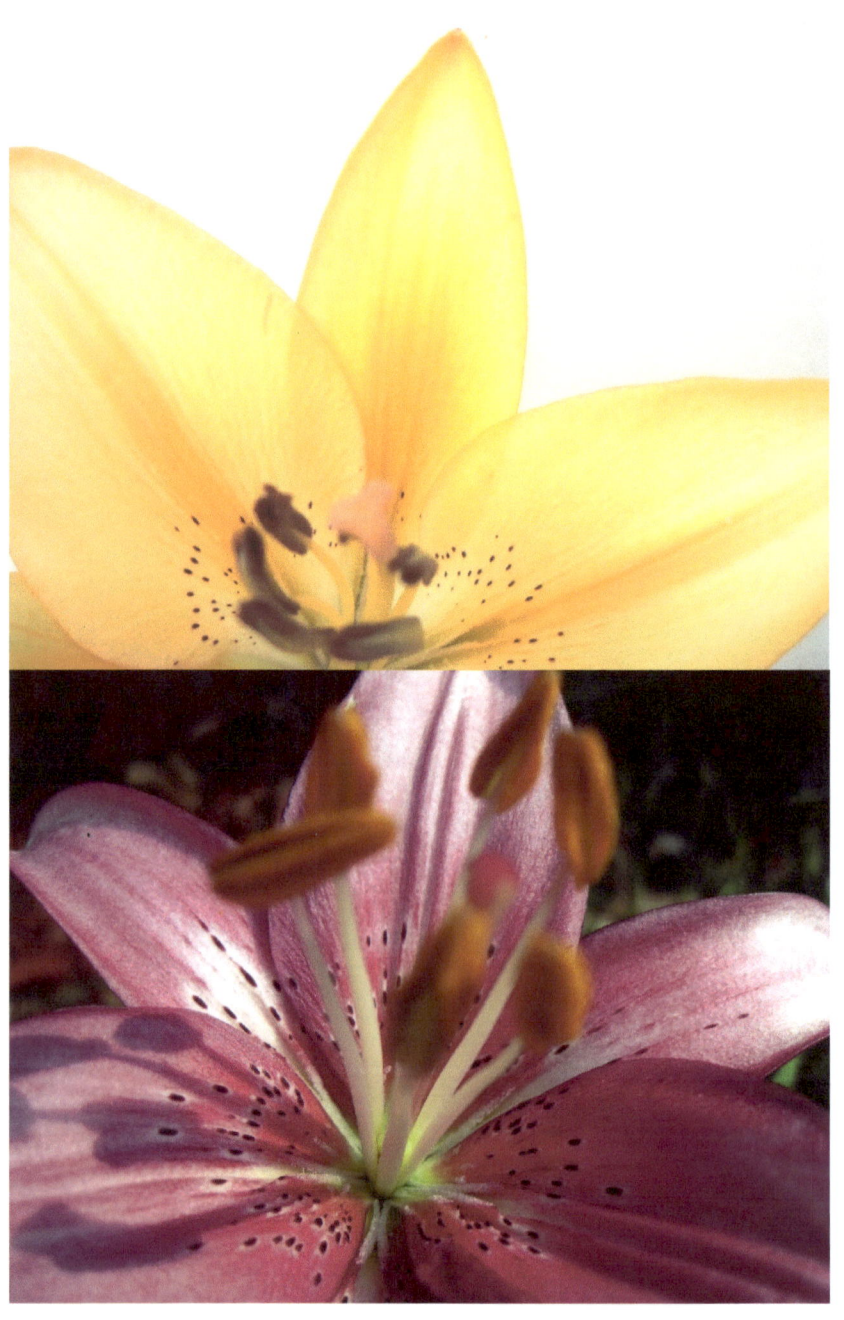

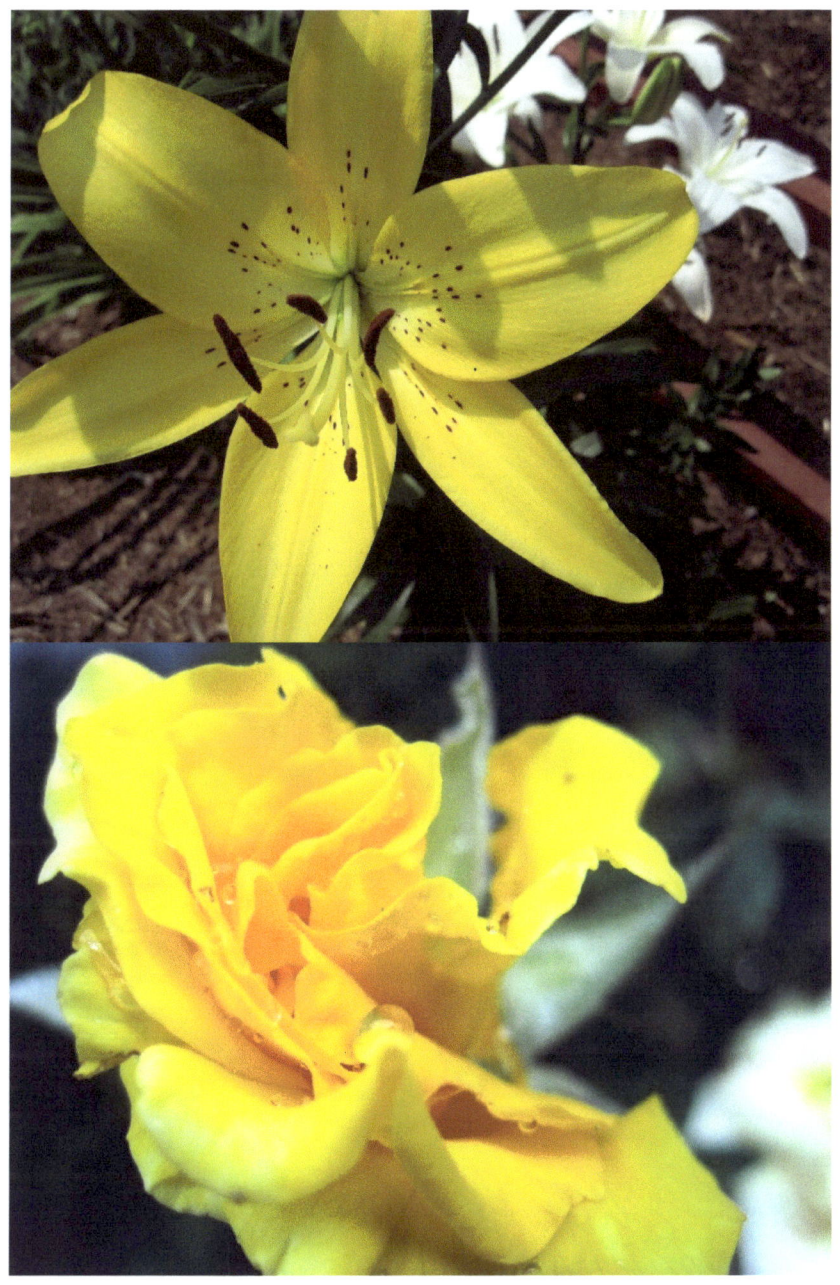

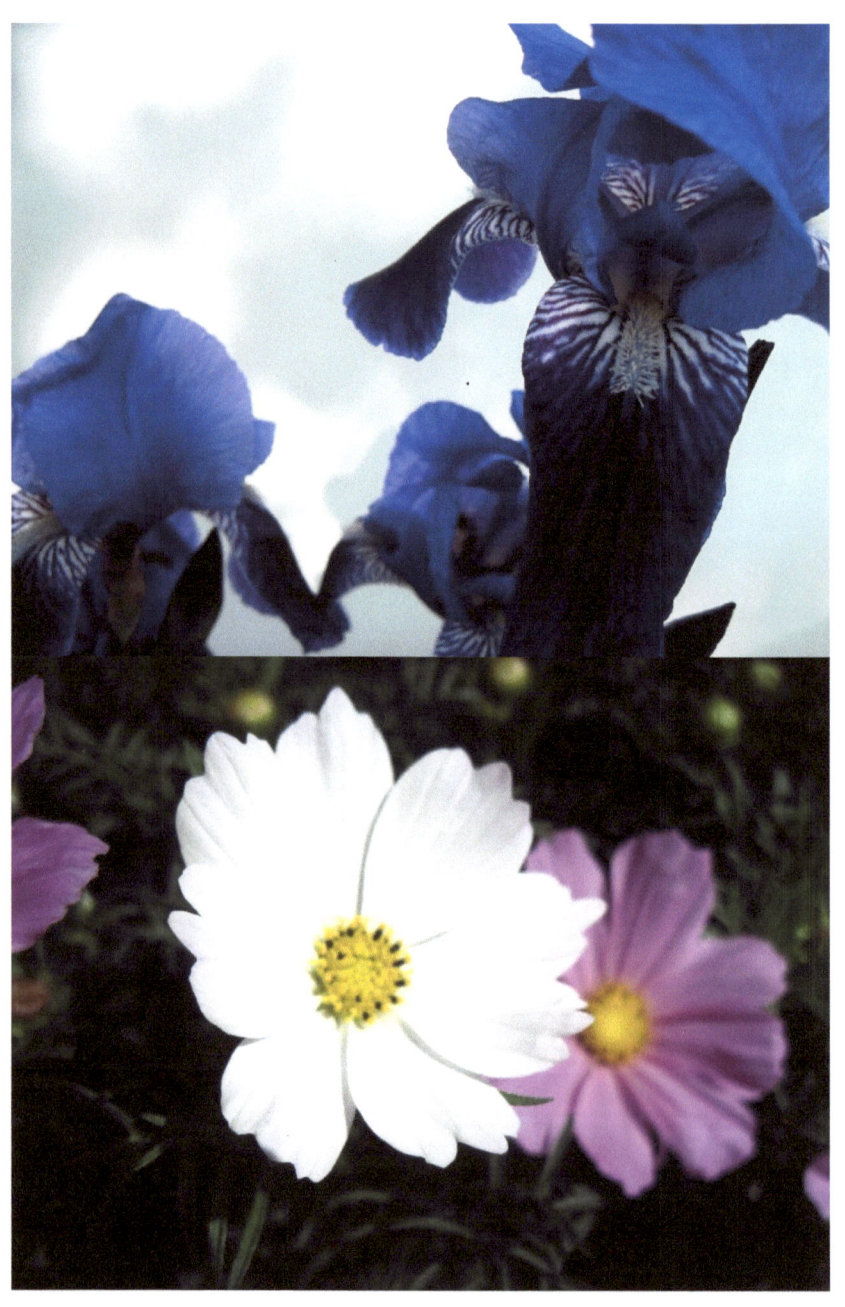

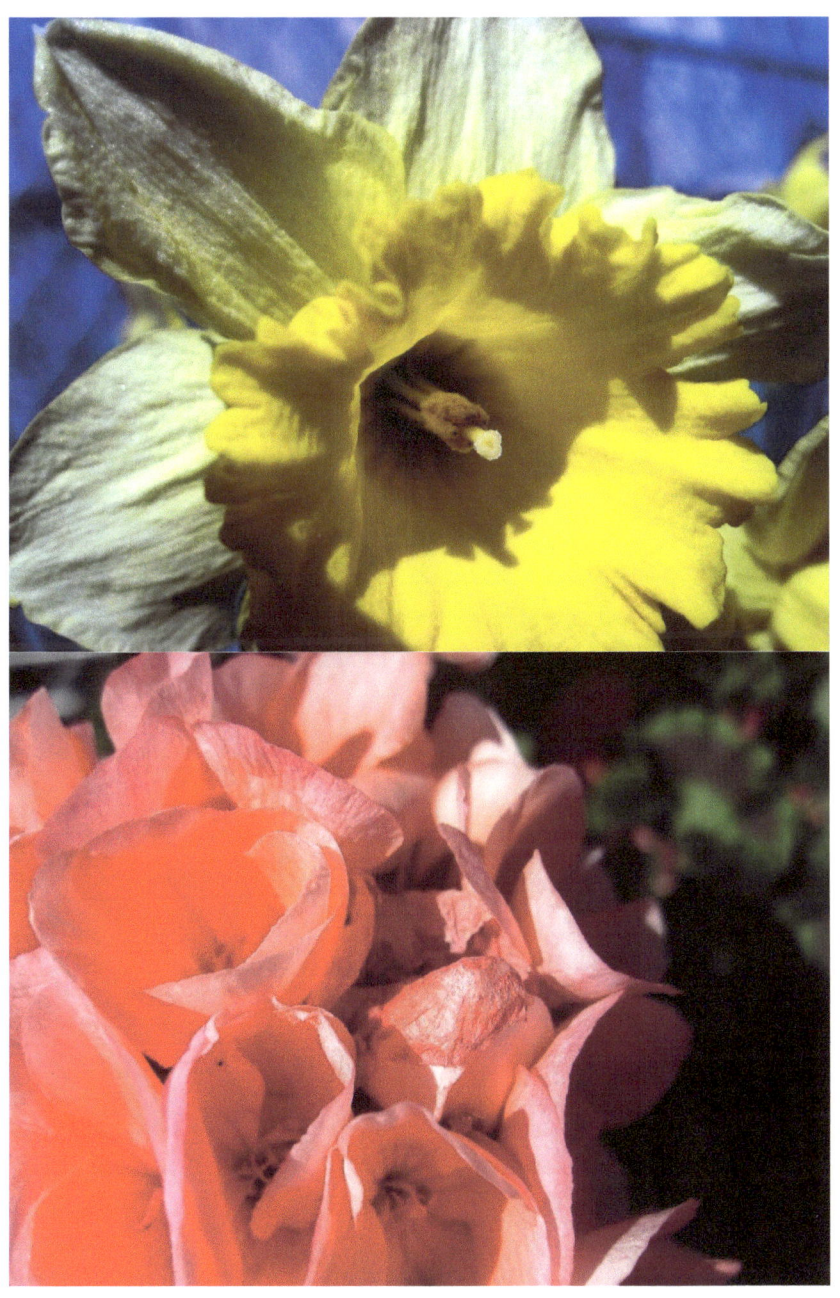

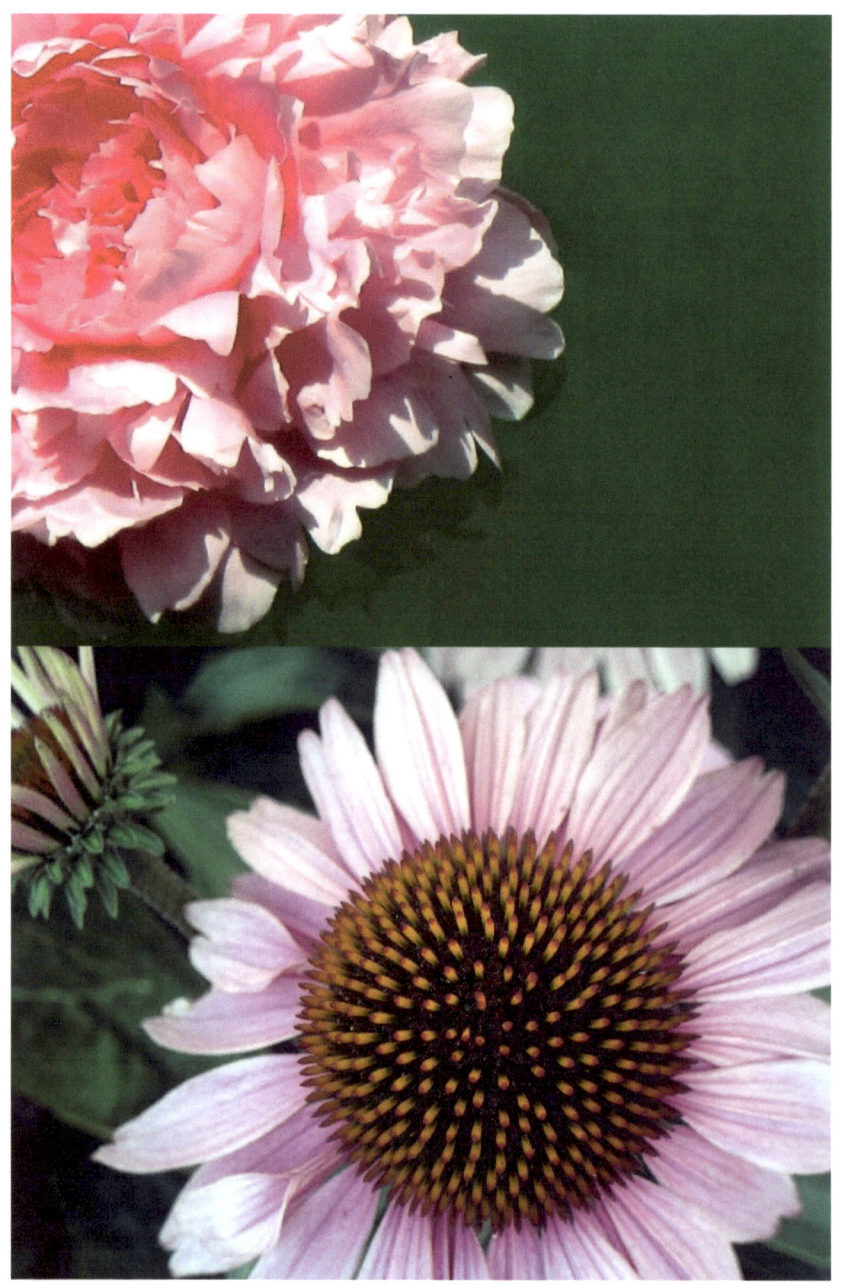

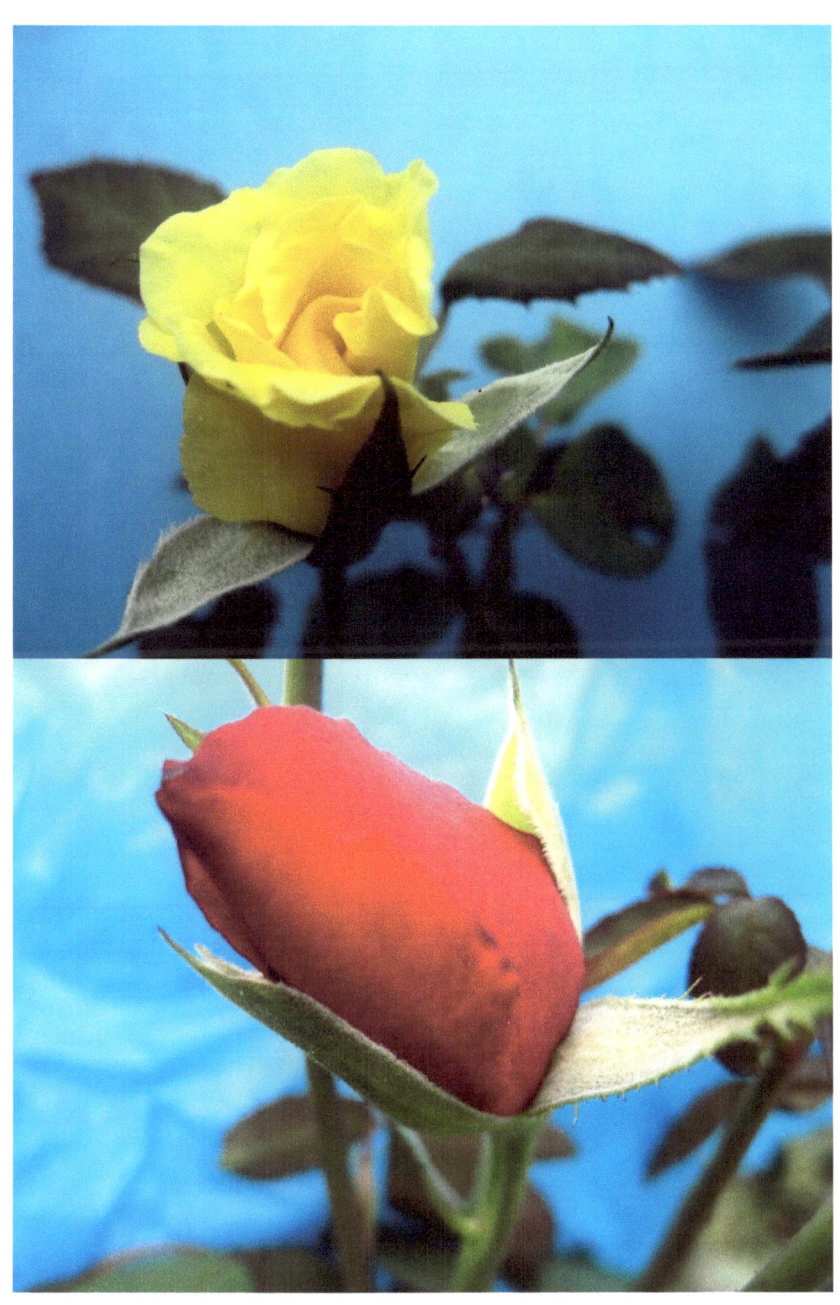

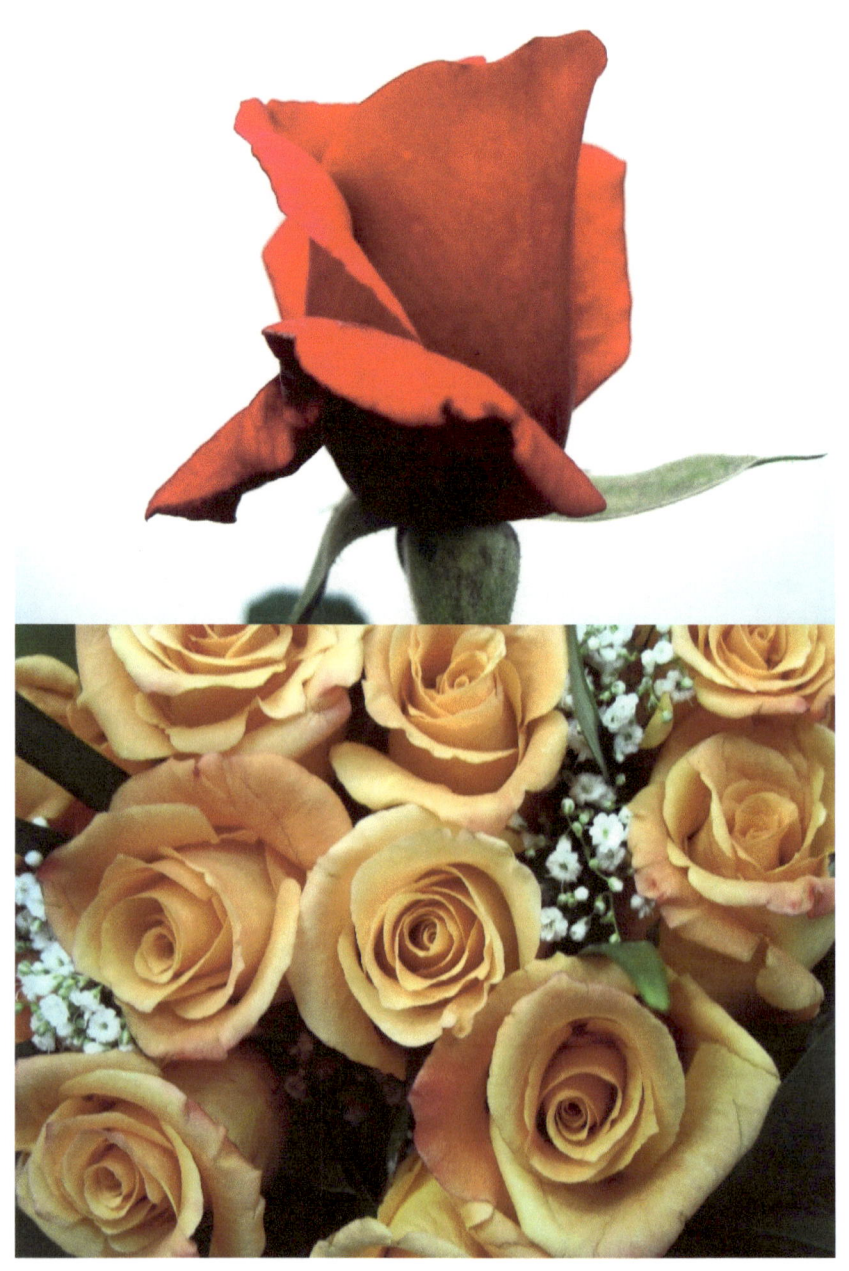

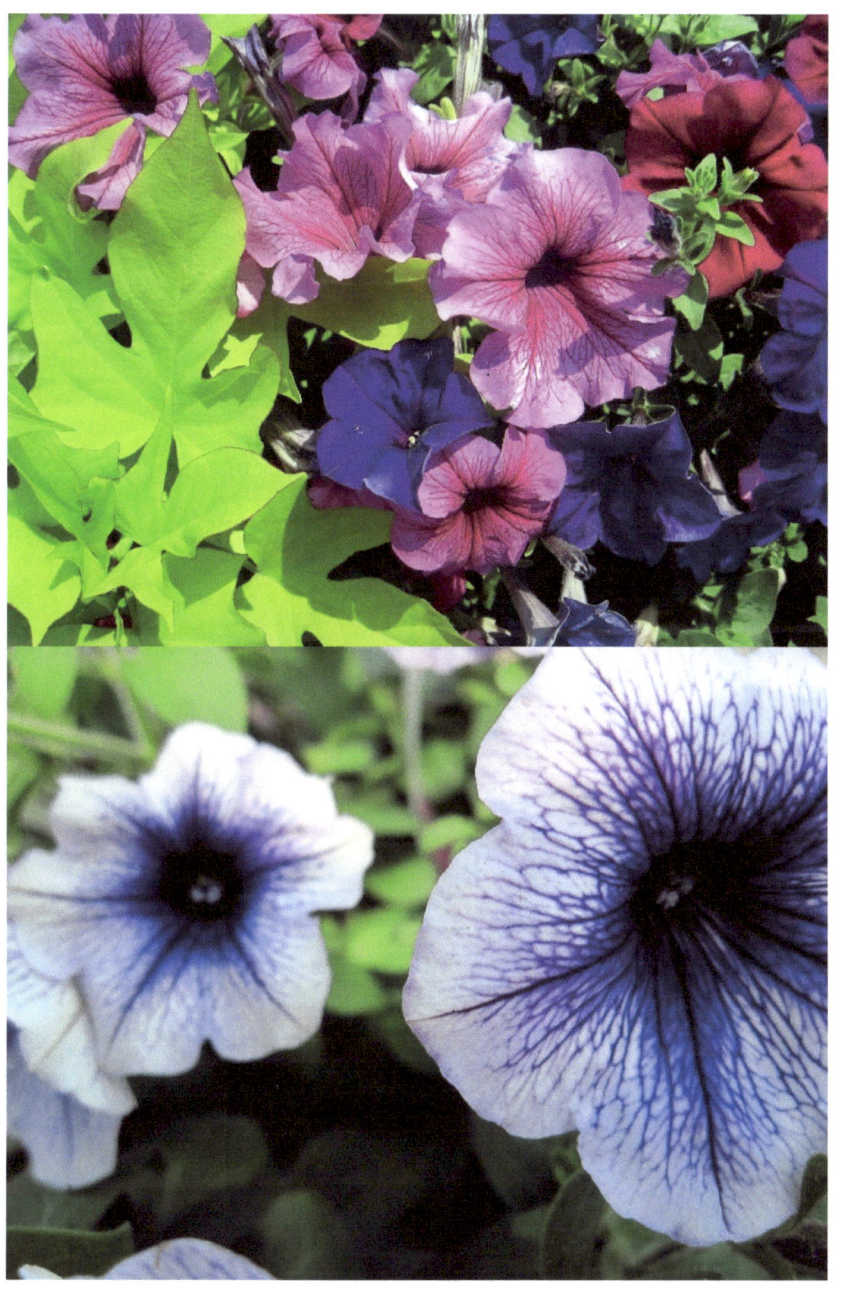

www.ingramcontent.com/pod-product-compliance
Lightning Source LLC
Chambersburg PA
CBHW041621180526
45159CB00002BC/956